Sea Without a Shore

To the children of Bermuda—B.R.

For Tristan—K.R.

For information about permission to reproduce selections from this book, write to Permissions,
W. W. Norton & Company, Inc., 500 Fifth Avenue, New York, NY 10110

For information about special discounts for bulk purchases, please contact W. W. Norton Special
Sales at specialsales@wwnorton.com or 800-233-4830

Manufacturing by RRD Asia
Book design by Hana Anouk Nakamura
Production manager: Delaney Adams

ISBN: 978-1-324-01607-6

W. W. Norton & Company, Inc.
500 Fifth Avenue, New York, N.Y. 10110
www.wwnorton.com

W. W. Norton & Company Ltd.
15 Carlisle Street, London W1D 3BS

1 2 3 4 5 6 7 8 9 0

Sea Without a Shore
Life in the Sargasso

Barb Rosenstock

illustrated by
Katherine Roy

Norton Young Readers
An Imprint of W. W. Norton & Company
Independent Publishers Since 1923

In the middle of nowhere,
hundreds of miles into the Atlantic Ocean,
five currents swirl billions of gallons of water clockwise
around and around

into the Sargasso Sea—saltier, warmer, and two feet higher in the center than the ocean that surrounds it. The only sea on Earth without a shore. A blue desert—hardly any food, even less shelter . . .

except where rafts of seaweed roll on the surface. Sargassum—an algae, not a plant. Instead of stems and leaves, it grows stipes and blades. Gas-filled globes keep the weed on the surface. In the middle of this sea, Sargassum develops no roots, no flowers, no seeds;

but still finds a way to start over.

If a tip of old weed breaks, a young seaweed begins.
Small and alone in a vast sweep of water.

It lives. Changing sunlight into sugars.

It spreads. One stipe, one blade, one globe at a time.

It tumbles. Surfing the waves.

Circling with the currents,
floating around and around
turning into
a sturdy place . . .

for tiny creatures to settle.

Crusty bryozoans.
Feathery hydroids.
Spiraled tube worms.

They cling. Settling the weed by chance.
Squirting chemicals or minerals that stick fast.
They build. Shape by shape. Circles, hexagons, cylinders.

They stay. Forever part of this place.
Defending, reproducing, expanding.
Filtering the water. Feeding on the
microscopic life that surrounds them.

Covering the weed,
which keeps floating,
around and around,
turning into
a fertile place . . .

for slow creatures to graze.

Rubbery snails.
Waving anemones.
Spongy nudibranchs.

They sense. Motion or chemicals.
Using eyes, receptors, or tentacles.

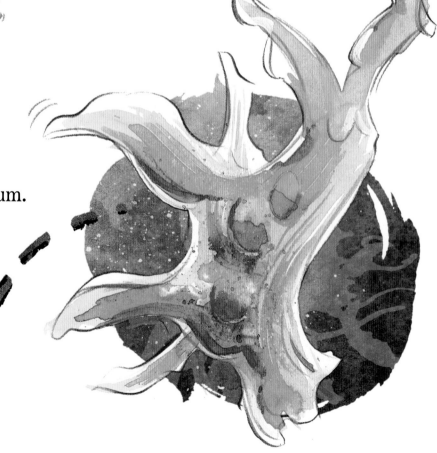

They stalk. Scraping or stinging.
Coaxing prey toward toothless,
pulsing mouths.
They eat. Muscles squeeze and cells
absorb. Over again; in then out.

Making waste. Feeding the Sargassum.
Avoiding hungry neighbors.

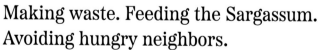

Cowering in the weed,
which keeps floating,
around and around,
turning into
a mysterious place . . .

for wandering creatures to explore.

    Pinching crabs.
        Skittering shrimp.
            Buggy amphipods.

They search. Paddling on jointed legs. In five or seven pairs.
They hide. Some disappear in the water. Others change color to mimic the weed patch.
They scavenge. Snatching and shredding. A fin here, a shell there.
Gobbling living, dead—plants, animals, and odd stuff in-between.

Cleaning up the weed,
which keeps floating,
around and around,
turning into
a challenging place . . .

for young creatures to grow.

Pointy swordfish.
Stocky jacks.
Blunt-nosed mahi-mahi.

They cluster. Nibbling scraps bobbing in the water. Chasing morsels fallen from the weed.

They scatter. Dodging up, down, left, right. As hungry adults circle, chase, and bite. Watch out!

They swim. And never stop—
through cloudless calms and
shocking storms. Day by night by
day teeth sharpen, fins toughen,
tails grow powerful.

Changing with the weed,
which keeps floating,
around and around
turning into
a unique place . . .

for weird creatures to survive.

Toothless pipefish.
Riffling flatworm.
Crawling frogfish.

The pipefish vacuums. Sucking up amphipods.
Waving in the water like a blade on a stipe.
The flatworm slinks. Breathing through its skin.
Regrowing body parts when needed.
The frogfish creeps. Hanging by fingery fins.
Luring in prey, darting out to swallow it whole.
Of all the special places on Earth, they, and others,
can live only here in the Sargasso.

Counting on the weed,
which keeps floating,
around and around
turning into
a diverse place . . .

for Earth's creatures to visit.

Insect.
Reptile.
Bird.
Fish.
Mammal.

Just born. Already grown. Seen or unseen.
Some from miles away. Others from the weed raft next door.

Water-striders speed on the surface past
hatchling turtles basking in the hot sun.
Flying fish eggs hatch from bubble nests
as silvery marlin roam in cool shadows.
Sooty terns and storm petrels circle above.
Humpback whales and tiger sharks migrate below.

In the middle of nowhere, a community thrives.
Season by season. Year after year. Age to age. Life into life.

Because a patch of seaweed
you could hold in your hand
keeps floating,
around and around,
until it turns into
the perfect place . . .

Home.

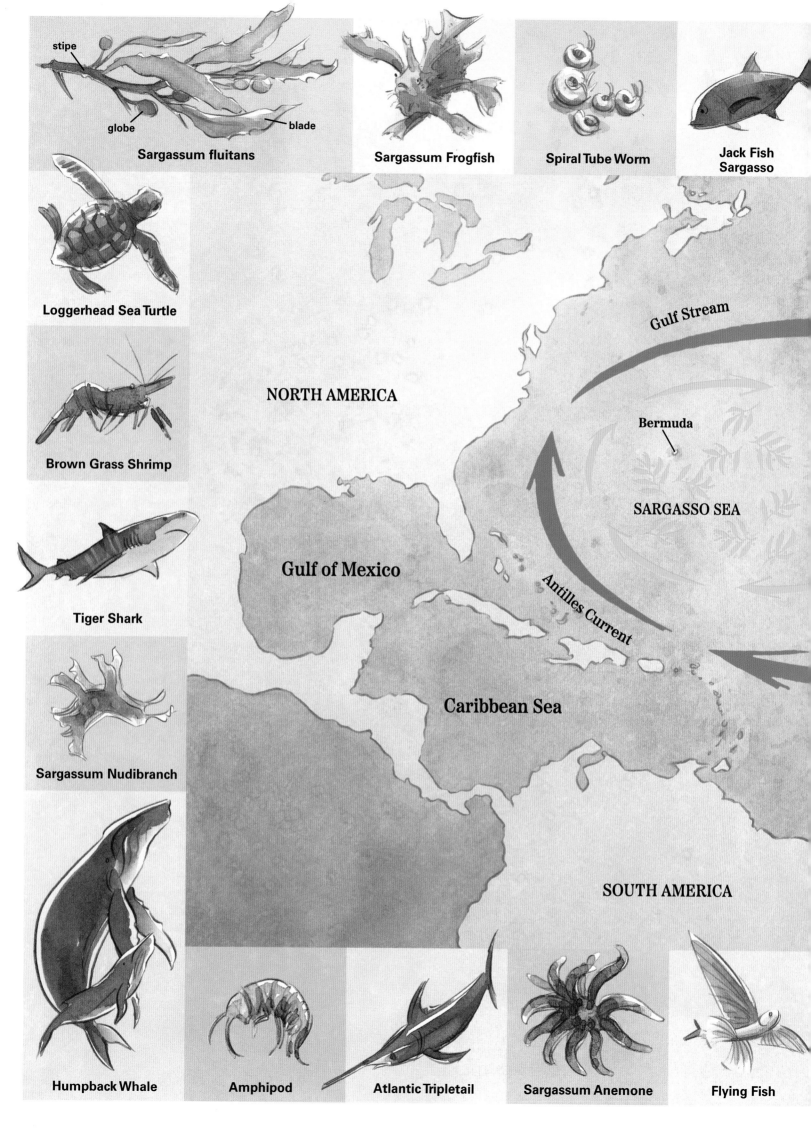

Sargassum fluitans
stipe
globe
blade

Sargassum Frogfish

Spiral Tube Worm

Jack Fish Sargasso

Loggerhead Sea Turtle

Brown Grass Shrimp

Tiger Shark

Sargassum Nudibranch

Humpback Whale

Amphipod

Atlantic Tripletail

Sargassum Anemone

Flying Fish

NORTH AMERICA

Gulf Stream

Bermuda

SARGASSO SEA

Gulf of Mexico

Antilles Current

Caribbean Sea

SOUTH AMERICA

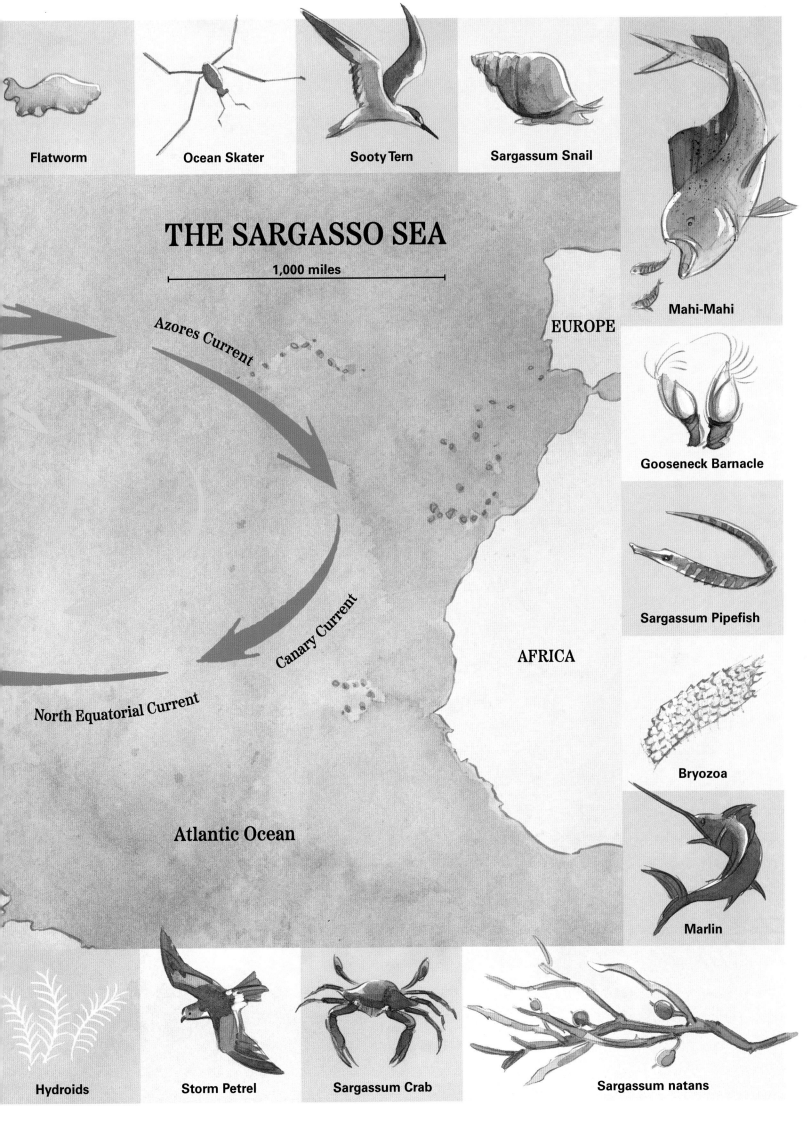

Flatworm

Ocean Skater

Sooty Tern

Sargassum Snail

Mahi-Mahi

Gooseneck Barnacle

Sargassum Pipefish

Bryozoa

Marlin

THE SARGASSO SEA

1,000 miles

Azores Current

EUROPE

Canary Current

AFRICA

North Equatorial Current

Atlantic Ocean

Hydroids

Storm Petrel

Sargassum Crab

Sargassum natans

AFTERWORD

This book has taken you on a journey through the ocean's floating golden rainforest, the Sargasso Sea, into the warm middle of the Atlantic Ocean, where thousands of wondrous creatures live among the lacy fronds of drifting Sargassum seaweed. Now you know! For some, such as the lumpy Sargassum fish and the sleek Sargassum shrimp, this is their only home. Baby sea turtles, tunas, and flying fish are sheltered here, curious dolphins, sharks, and whales stop by to visit, while luminous jellies and other deep-sea animals swim in the depths below.

With knowing comes caring, and with caring there is hope that the amazing diversity of life in the Sargasso Sea will be forever protected. Like trees on the land, Sargassum forests generate oxygen and capture carbon dioxide, doing their part in maintaining the systems that make Earth habitable for sea creatures—and for life on the land as well—including you!

All life on Earth depends on a healthy ocean, and learning about it, loving it, and protecting it is important to everyone, everywhere, all the time.

—Sylvia Earle

Dr. Sylvia Earle is president and chairman of Mission Blue, an Explorer-in-Residence at the National Geographic Society, founder of Deep Ocean Exploration and Research, Inc. (DOER), chair of the Advisory Council for the Harte Research Institute, former chief scientist of NOAA, and the author of more than 225 publications and leader of more than 100 expeditions with over 7,500 hours underwater. She has received more than 100 national and international honors and awards, including being named *Time* magazine's first Hero for the Planet.

A cluster of Sargassum (Sargassum fluitans) from a beach in Bermuda.

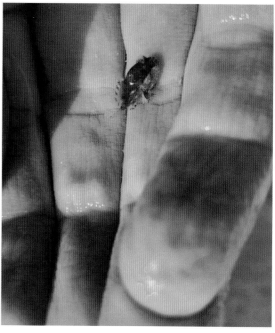

A Sargassum frogfish (Histrio histrio) found hidden in a clump of Sargassum weed. Tiny, yet ferocious, the frogfish hangs on to the weed waiting to gulp down prey whole (notice it hanging on to Katherine's fingers!) Histrio histrio is found only in the Sargasso Sea.

RESEARCH NOTE

In January of 2019, Barb tripped on a tangle of drying seaweed on a beach in the Dominican Republic. She learned it was called Sargassum and came from a part of the Atlantic Ocean called the Sargasso Sea—an area about 2,000 miles long, 700 miles wide, and on average almost 12,000 feet deep. Thousands of creatures depend in some way on this Sargassum seaweed, which is *holopelagic*, meaning it lives in open ocean, and reproduces through *fragmentation*: splitting into pieces, each of which develops into a fully grown individual that is a clone of the original. The weed depends on the nutrients produced by its community, as well as the quality of the ocean's water, and the earth's climate. Barb also learned (after many drafts) that it is nearly impossible to fit all the life in the Sargasso into one picture book. So, she focused the story on a new seaweed fragment and its growing community.

In early May 2022, Barb and Katherine went on a research trip to Bermuda, the only landmass located within the Sargasso Sea. There, they met up with two oceanographers, Dr. Kerry Whittaker and Dr. Robbie Smith, to learn more about "the weed that feeds the North Atlantic."* After dinner at Dr. Smith's home overlooking the beach, they held fresh Sargassum for the first time. The oceanographers pointed out different *hydroids* (an anemone-like stage in the life of small animals related to jellyfish) and *bryozoans* (tiny invertebrate animals that live as colonies in mineral skeletons, like corals) on the weed. The next day the scientists guided Barb and Katherine through a variety of ocean-life exhibits at the Bermuda Aquarium, Museum & Zoo. Together, they examined preserved specimens of seaweed species along with mollusks including *nudibranchs* (a soft-bodied, shell-less mollusk, part of the sea slug family) and other life-forms that are *endemic* to the Sargasso—able to live only there. The oceanographers took Barb and Katherine snorkeling to get a sense of Bermuda's underwater habitat and a closer look at some of the corals and larger fish.

Katherine brought watercolors on the trip, and began testing hues to find the specific, clear blue of the Sargasso Sea. Winsor blue was the best match for the color of the deep water, and lemon-yellow mixed with a little natural sienna and cadmium scarlet were a good fit to represent the range of color for the weed at the surface. On the last day, Dr. Smith and Dr. Whittaker took Katherine and Barb out in a boat. They netted soccer ball–sized clumps of Sargassum, examining each one for any hidden passengers in the weed. They found crabs, flatworms, skittering shrimp, a mysterious clump of eggs, and best of all, two *Histrio histrio*—the famous Sargasso "frogfish" that climbs through the weed on its modified fins. Before returning home, Katherine sketched out rough composition plans for the final art while Barb added new information and impressions to the text. The Sargasso had worked its curious magic on both author and illustrator, and hopefully it will work its magic on you.

A single clump of Sargassum can live for decades, and it's estimated that the Sargasso Sea has existed for ten thousand years. Human action (and inaction) is rapidly changing this ancient balance of life. Overfishing and wasteful fishing result in decreased fish populations. Other risks come from plastic pollution, ship traffic, and oil, chemical, or sewage spills. It is up to us to protect this home for so many creatures. Anything that helps the Sargasso Sea thrive helps the general health of the oceans, and all life on our connected planet.

*James Prosek, *National Geographic* 235, no. 6 (June 2019): 126.

TOO MUCH SARGASSUM?

Small amounts of Sargassum weed normally drift onto beaches and naturally decay, providing nourishment to coastal habitats. But starting in 2011, unusually large amounts of Sargassum weed, called *inundations*, began washing up on beaches in the Caribbean, Mexico, and Florida. As the large patches of seaweed rot, they release increased amounts of a smelly, sulfur gas that can choke beach ecosystems, impact businesses, and make some people sick.

 Ocean scientists are studying the reasons for these continuing Sargassum inundations. Early data suggest a number of potential causes, including warming water, changing winds, and altered currents due to climate change, and industrial farm fertilizer runoff and dust clouds from the Sahara, both of which contain chemicals that enter the ocean and overfeed the seaweed.

 Sargassum is essential ocean habitat. Yet the news media often covers seaweed as a threat, even though most causes of too much Sargassum are under human control. For more information on the importance of Sargassum and the Sargasso Sea, visit sargassoseacommission.org.

ACKNOWLEDGMENTS

This book could not have been written without the deep knowledge of Dr. Kerry Whittaker, assistant professor, Corning School of Oceanography, Maine Maritime Academy, and Dr. Robbie Smith, curator, Bermuda Natural History Museum. Thanks also to: Dr. Jeff Schell, professor of oceanography; Dr. Porter Hoagland, oceanographer emeritus, and the staff of the Sea Education Association program at Woods Hole Oceanographic Institution; Dr. Amy Siuda, associate professor of marine science, Eckerd College; Dr. Kate Mansfield, associate professor, biological sciences, University of Central Florida; and David Freestone of the Sargasso Sea Commission.

SOURCES

Dozens of research sources were consulted, the most important include:

Butler, J. N., Morris, B. F., Cadwallader, J., and Stoner, A. W., *Studies of Sargassum and the Sargassum Community*, Bermuda Biological Station, Special Publication No. 22, 1983.

Laffoley, D. d'A, Roe, H. S. J., Angel, M. V., et al., *The Protection and Management of the Sargasso Sea: The Golden Floating Rainforest of the Atlantic Ocean*, Bermuda, Sargasso Sea Alliance, 2011.

Morris, B. F., and Mogelberg, D. D., *Identification Manual to the Pelagic Sargassum Fauna*, Bermuda Biological Station for Research, Special Publication No. 11, 1973.

Woods Hole Oceanographic Institution, Sea Education Association (SEA), *Ocean Literacy for Remote Ocean Regions*, Marine Biodiversity and Conservation Symposium, June 23–24, 2019.

For a complete source list, please visit www.barbrosenstock.com.